The World at Night

EDITED BY JOSEPHINE SOUTHON
DESIGNED BY DERRIAN BRADDER
COVER DESIGNED BY ANGIE ALLISON

CONSULTANCY BY CAMILLA DE LA BEDOYERE AND STUART ATKINSON

WITH SPECIAL THANKS TO BRYONY DAVIES

To Wilbur – B.L.

For Sami. Don't be afraid of the darkness,
but look at the wonder it brings. Titi, Aito and
I will always leave a light on for you – P.B.

First published in Great Britain in 2025 by Buster Books,
an imprint of Michael O'Mara Books Limited, 9 Lion Yard,
Tremadoc Road, London SW4 7NQ

W www.mombooks.com/buster   f Buster Books   🐦 @BusterBooks   📷 @buster_books

A CIP catalogue record for this book is available from the British Library.

ISBN: 978-1-78055-933-9

1 3 5 7 9 10 8 6 4 2

This book was printed in December 2024 by
Shenzhen Wing King Tong Paper Products Co. Ltd.,
Shenzhen, Guangdong, China.

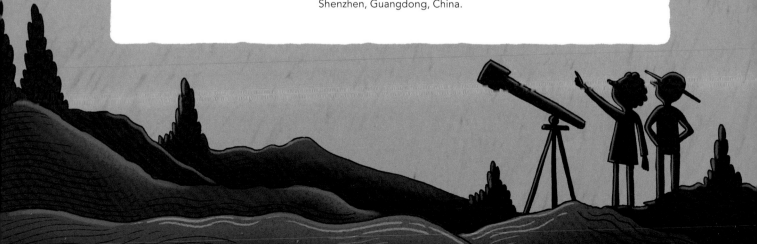

The World at Night

BUSTER BOOKS

WRITTEN BY BEN LERWILL
ILLUSTRATED BY PAULA BOSSIO

CONTENTS

INTRODUCTION

Night is a magical, mysterious time. Daylight has disappeared and the world feels slower and calmer. There's a scattering of stars in the sky and a whisper of wind in the trees. But wait ...

Have you ever wondered what's going on out there in the darkness, while you're tucked up in bed? Are animals still scurrying around? Are people still working? And what's happening in places far away?

The planet at night isn't as quiet as it seems. And even when you're asleep, the lands and seas outside your bedroom are WILDLY alive.

This book is a celebration of life after sunset. It looks at why we have night, why we need sleep and why we dream. It points a telescope at the night sky, follows the Moon through its monthly phases and shows people performing vital jobs right through the night. It looks at life in the dark polar winters, explores the history of electric light and explains why solar eclipses can feel like night.

And that's not all. Night might be a time of rest for *most* of us humans, but for countless animal species it's when they're busiest. Ever since the earliest prehistoric mammals shifted their activity away from the daytime to avoid hungry dinosaurs, the hours of darkness have been crawling with wonderful creatures.

Today, two thirds of mammals – and all manner of birds, amphibians, reptiles, fish and insects – are nocturnal, which means they are active at night. This book shines a torch on these fascinating species, travelling from the jungles of South America and the icefields of Antarctica to the dunes of the Arabian Desert and the waters of the Great Barrier Reef. How do these animals see in the gloom? What do they eat? When do they sleep?

The following pages answer all these questions, and many more. So, as the curtain of darkness falls once more over the planet, let's discover THE WORLD AT NIGHT.

AS DAY TURNS TO NIGHT ...

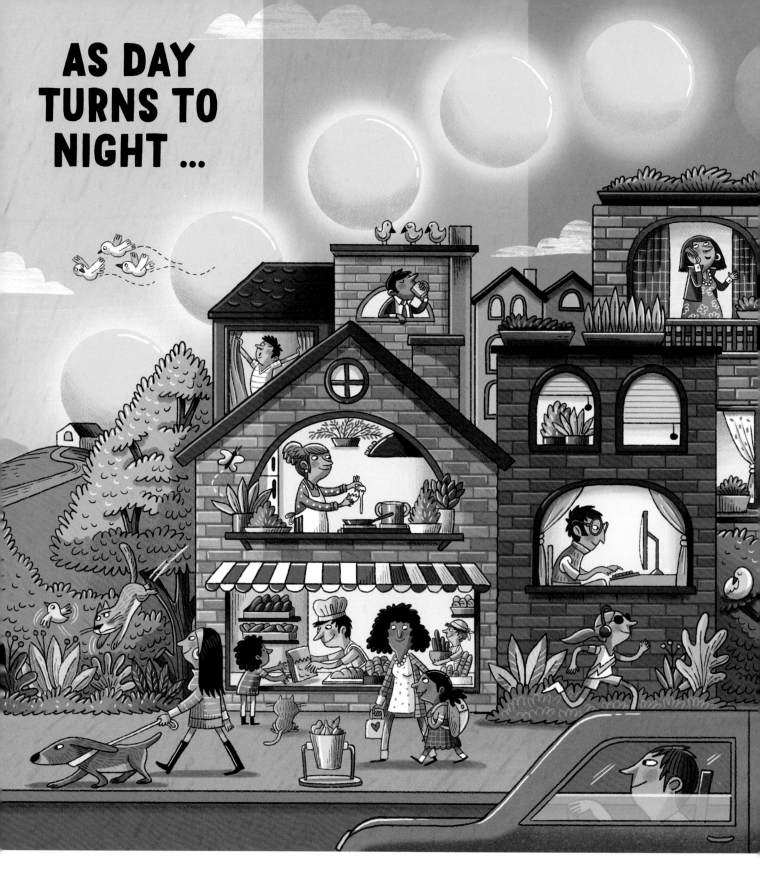

It's dawn. The Sun is rising above the horizon, greeting the start of a new day. Birds are singing, alarms are sounding and curtains are drawn open. The world is slowly waking up – and warming up – for another busy day.

As people leave home to set off for work or school, the streets and roads start to fill. Dog-walkers and joggers appear on the pavements. The smell of freshly baked bread drifts from bakeries. The day is brighter now, and noisier.

Most of us experience every single day of our lives beneath the natural light of the Sun. As morning becomes afternoon and afternoon becomes evening, our routine is synchronized with the Sun's journey across the sky.

As the Sun dips towards the horizon, the temperature drops and the sky loses its glow. This time of day is called dusk. For many of us, this is a chance to wind down, enjoy an evening meal and relax.

The last of the colour fades from the sky. Stars appear overhead and streetlights flicker on along the roads. As you get ready for bed, the world outside feels emptier and quieter than during the day. But is it?

With darkness settling in, new creatures emerge from the shadows. A different cast of human characters appears, too, heading off to begin work. Night has arrived, but the planet is still bursting with life.

WHAT IS NIGHT?

It might seem obvious what night is. It's when it gets dark, right? But why does it get dark in the first place? And why do different parts of the world experience night at different times?

EARTH'S ROTATION

As our planet makes its year-long journey around the Sun, it spins slowly on its **axis** – an imaginary rod that runs from the North Pole to the South Pole. As each part of the world rotates away from the Sun, daylight disappears and darkness arrives. Night-time lasts until that part of the planet turns to face the Sun again, at sunrise. The Earth completes one full spin on its axis every 24 hours.

CAIRO, EGYPT

SAN FRANCISCO, USA

Right now, while you're reading this book, half of the Earth's surface is facing towards the darkness of space, while the other half is lit by the Sun's glow. For example, Cairo in Egypt is on the other side of the world to San Francisco in the USA. This means that when the Sun has set in Cairo, it's rising in San Francisco, thousands of miles away. Much later, when the Sun sets in San Francisco, it will rise shortly after in Cairo.

HOW DO OTHER PLANETS EXPERIENCE NIGHT?

Each of the planets in our Solar System spins on its own axis, so they experience night and day, too. The planets are all turning at different speeds, which determines the length of their days and nights. So how long is a day–night cycle on other planets?

MERCURY
1 cycle = 1,408 hours

VENUS
1 cycle = 5,832 hours

EARTH
1 cycle = 24 hours

MARS
1 cycle = 25 hours

JUPITER
1 cycle = 10 hours

SATURN
1 cycle = 11 hours

URANUS
1 cycle = 17 hours

NEPTUNE
1 cycle = 16 hours

A TIME TO REST, OR TO ROAM?

Day and night have always been part of life on Earth. For millions of years, humans have witnessed the Sun rising and falling each day, just as you do now.

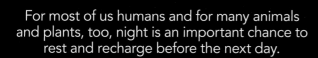

For most of us humans and for many animals and plants, too, night is an important chance to rest and recharge before the next day.

But for lots of others, the darkness offers a vital opportunity to hunt, to hide, to work or to make new discoveries. It's a time to thrive and survive.

THE DAY–NIGHT CYCLE

Each day–night cycle on Earth lasts 24 hours, but not every day and night are the same length. They vary depending on the time of year, and where you are in the world.

During our annual journey around the Sun – which takes 365 days, or 365 Earth-spins – the world is tilted on its axis. This tilt creates our seasons, and affects the amount of darkness and daylight we have at different times of year.

Every year, our journey around the Sun is marked by four important dates.

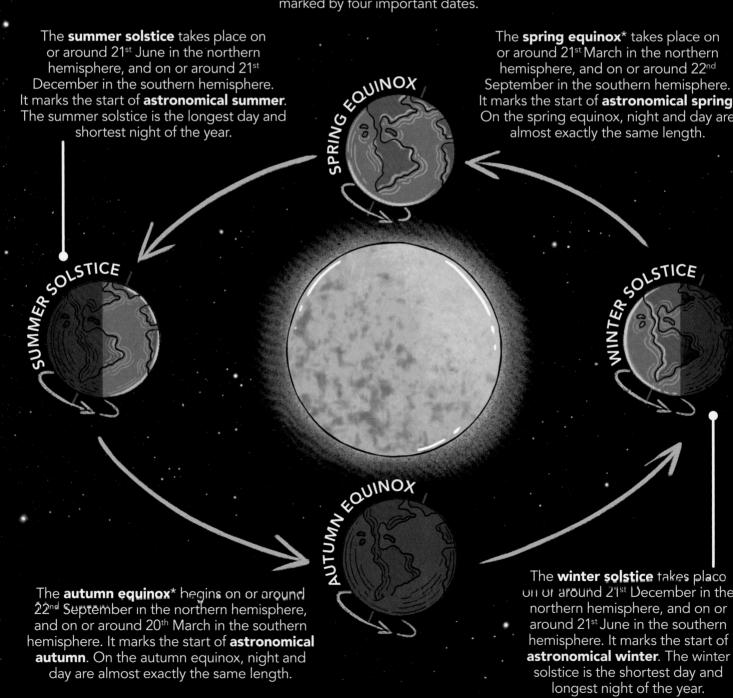

The **summer solstice** takes place on or around 21st June in the northern hemisphere, and on or around 21st December in the southern hemisphere. It marks the start of **astronomical summer**. The summer solstice is the longest day and shortest night of the year.

The **spring equinox*** takes place on or around 21st March in the northern hemisphere, and on or around 22nd September in the southern hemisphere. It marks the start of **astronomical spring**. On the spring equinox, night and day are almost exactly the same length.

SPRING EQUINOX

SUMMER SOLSTICE

WINTER SOLSTICE

AUTUMN EQUINOX

The **autumn equinox*** begins on or around 22nd September in the northern hemisphere, and on or around 20th March in the southern hemisphere. It marks the start of **astronomical autumn**. On the autumn equinox, night and day are almost exactly the same length.

The **winter solstice** takes place on or around 21st December in the northern hemisphere, and on or around 21st June in the southern hemisphere. It marks the start of **astronomical winter**. The winter solstice is the shortest day and longest night of the year.

*The word 'equinox' is Latin for 'equal night'.

Countries above the equator in the northern hemisphere, such as France, are tilted towards the Sun in June, July and August. They receive more direct sunlight in these months, so this is when they experience summer, with long days and short nights.

But in December, January and February, the same countries are tilted AWAY from the Sun. This is when they experience winter, with long nights and short days.

PARIS, FRANCE

For countries below the equator, in the southern hemisphere, the opposite is true. When it's summer in the north of the world, it's winter in the south of the world – and vice versa.

What about countries ON the equator, such as Kenya? Because of where they're located in relation to the Sun, they have 12-hour days and 12-hour nights all year round.

MAASAI MARA NATIONAL RESERVE, KENYA

LOFOTEN, NORWAY

Things are very different in the polar regions at the top and bottom of the globe, such as Norway. The North and South Poles have seasons when the Sun doesn't rise at all, and other seasons when it doesn't set. This means night-time in winter – or daytime in summer – can last several months!

THE NIGHT SKY

There's nothing quite so magical as a clear, starry night, when the clouds roll back to reveal the glittering vastness of the Milky Way. Far away from city lights, it's sometimes possible to look up and count thousands of stars – some just faint glimmers, others as bright as jewels. When we gaze up at them, we're staring across trillions of kilometres of space. It can make our own world feel tiny. There's so much to be discovered about the stars and Moon above our heads – let's find out more.

STARGAZING

When you stargaze, you're looking back in time. Our galaxy is so big that the light from stars can take hundreds of years or more to reach us here on Earth.

ASTRONOMY

Humans have always been fascinated by the night sky. The study of stars and the universe is called astronomy.

Three thousand years ago, ancient Babylonians were the first to record the movement and patterns of the stars and planets across the heavens. Temple scribes engraved their findings on clay tablets.

With the telescope's invention in 17th-century Europe, astronomers spotted new details in the night sky, like the Moon's craters and Saturn's rings. Since then, humans have discovered many more incredible things.

WHAT CAN YOU SEE?

From certain areas on Earth, a clear night sky can bring spectacular sights.

Shooting stars aren't actually stars but small rocks called **meteors**, burning up as they enter our atmosphere. Ancient cultures used myths to explain shooting stars. In Britain, people believed they were souls returning to Earth.

There are two trillion **galaxies** in the universe. We live in one called **the Milky Way**, which contains at least 100 billion stars. From our side-on view on Earth, it looks like a long band in the sky. The Milky Way is actually spiral-shaped.

EARTH

Space technology is always advancing. Powerful **space telescopes** take incredibly detailed images of distant stars, galaxies and glowing gas clouds called nebulae. Special **observatories** and **planetariums** around the world allow people to use advanced stargazing equipment, and learn more about the night sky from expert astronomers.

CONSTELLATIONS

Some groups of stars form patterns that we call constellations. There are 88 of them in total, and they help us to understand the night sky. Here are five of the easiest constellations you can spot on a clear night. You won't even need a telescope!

ORION

This constellation resembles a hunter from Greek mythology. The pattern is well-known for the row of three stars that form Orion's Belt. From Earth, it looks like they form a line but the middle star in the belt is nearly twice as far away as the other two.

Where can I see Orion?
In parts of both hemispheres, from around November to February.

THE PLOUGH AND POLARIS

The Plough is part of a constellation called Ursa Major. It's a group of seven stars that looks like a saucepan. If you draw an imaginary line through the Plough's two far-right stars, it leads almost directly to Polaris. Also known as the North Star, Polaris can be found high above the North Pole.

Where can I see the Plough and Polaris?
Mainly in the northern hemisphere, year-round.

CASSIOPEIA

The 'W' shape of this constellation resembles the throne of arrogant Queen Cassiopeia from Greek mythology. According to legend, she was put in the sky as punishment for her boastfulness, to spin around the North Pole for eternity.

Where can I see Cassiopeia?
Mainly in the northern hemisphere, year-round.

THE SOUTHERN CROSS

The Southern Cross is the smallest constellation, but it's one of the easiest to identify. Its stars appear on the flags of many countries in the southern hemisphere, including Australia, New Zealand and Papua New Guinea.

Where can I see the Southern Cross?
In the southern hemisphere only, year-round.

TAURUS

Taurus is located near Orion. Also known as 'The Bull', its stars form the shape of a bull's head, chest and front legs. One of its star clusters, called the Pleiades, was used as an eye test in ancient times – if you could see all seven stars you had excellent vision.

Where can I see Taurus?
Mainly in the northern hemisphere, in winter.

YOU CAN SEE PLANETS FROM EARTH, TOO ...

With a telescope, it's also possible to spot the seven other planets in our Solar System. They're much nearer to us than stars, but they still look very far away.

Venus is always found fairly close to the Sun in the sky, before sunrise or after sunset. When it's visible in the west after sunset, it's known as the Evening Star.

Mars is known as the Red Planet. It can be recognized by its reddish tinge, caused by the iron oxide on its surface.

THE MOON

The Moon is almost 400,000 kilometres (249,000 miles) away, but it's our closest celestial neighbour.

Sometimes you can see its pale surface during the day – but it's much more visible when it's dark. Although this ball of dry rock is four times smaller than Earth, its bright glow can light up even the murkiest nights.

But the Moon doesn't produce its own light. The Sun is the only object in our Solar System that shines with its own light.

When you see the Moon shining, what you're actually looking at is light from the Sun, reflecting off the Moon and beaming back down towards you. We call this glow 'moonlight'.

HUMANS AND THE MOON

Nothing grows or lives on the Moon, but astronauts have walked on its crater-covered surface. The first two humans to land there were Neil Armstrong and Buzz Aldrin in 1969. Can you imagine looking back at Earth from all the way out there in space?

The Moon has many beliefs, traditions and celebrations attached to it. The Lantern Festival is celebrated in China on the first full Moon of the year. Paper lanterns are released into the night sky to symbolize hope for the coming year.

It's hard to see the Moon in the sky. The illuminated side faces away from the Earth completely.

A thin crescent of light on the right can be seen. 'Waxing' means it's getting bigger.

A thin crescent of light on the left can be seen. 'Waning' means it's getting smaller.

Half of the illuminated side on the right can be seen. We call this a 'half-moon'.

NEW MOON

WANING CRESCENT

WAXING CRESCENT

THE MONTHLY PHASES OF THE MOON

Like the Earth, the Moon has day and night. In other words, one side of the Moon is always illuminated by the Sun, and the other half is in the dark.

As the Moon orbits the Earth each month, it looks to us like its surface is changing shape. What we're actually seeing are different parts of the Moon being illuminated by the Sun. We call these changing views the eight 'phases'.

LAST QUARTER

FIRST QUARTER

WANING GIBBOUS

WAXING GIBBOUS

FULL MOON

Also known as the third quarter, half of the illuminated side on the left can be seen.

The Moon appears to start shrinking as it moves towards the Sun.

The illuminated side can be seen completely, for about two days.

Most of the illuminated side can be seen. 'Gibbous' means 'swollen'.

TOTAL SOLAR ECLIPSE

A solar eclipse occurs when the Moon blocks the view of the Sun from Earth. When the Moon only partly blocks the Sun's light, this is a **partial solar eclipse**. When the Sun is covered completely by the Moon, this is a **total solar eclipse**. For life on Earth, a total solar eclipse can feel like night-time.

WHY DOES IT HAPPEN?

The Moon orbits the Earth and the Earth orbits the Sun. When the Moon travels directly between the Earth and the Sun, it blocks the Sun from our view on Earth. The Moon is 400 times nearer to us than the Sun, but by sheer coincidence, it's also 400 times smaller. This means that when they're in line with each other, the Moon's outline fits exactly over the outline of the Sun.

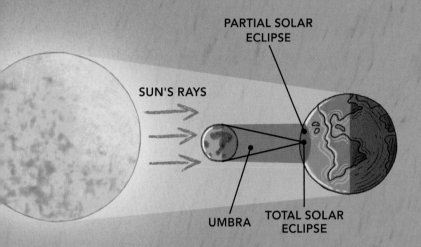

PARTIAL SOLAR ECLIPSE

SUN'S RAYS

UMBRA

TOTAL SOLAR ECLIPSE

The result is a few minutes of darkness for the part of Earth directly beneath the Moon's shadow (known as the **umbra**). Total solar eclipses are fascinating but rare – they only take place roughly every 18 months.

HOW CAN I SEE ONE?

You need to be standing in the correct place on Earth – the part that is covered by the centre of the Moon's shadow. If you're lucky enough to witness a total solar eclipse, it's important to wear special light-filtering glasses, otherwise the glare can damage your eyes.

ANIMALS AND PLANTS

Fascinatingly, wildlife often reacts to a total solar eclipse in the same way it reacts to night. Birds return to their roosts, cattle stop grazing, bats start flying, crickets start chirping and whales breach in the seas.

Plants that usually fold their petals in at night, like **hibiscus flowers**, start to close as if it were night-time.

LUNAR ECLIPSE

We also have lunar eclipses. These happen when a full Moon moves into Earth's shadow, where the Sun's rays can't reach it. During a total lunar eclipse, the Moon's white surface fades to a dark reddish colour – we call this a **Blood Moon**.

OCEANS

Let's sink into the deep dark blue. At night, the world's oceans are brimming with activity. Strange creatures emerge from under rocks to feed, nocturnal fish drift through the darkness and predators roam the seabed. Hundreds of thousands of different species live below the waves – and for many of them, life begins at sundown.

TEMPERATE OCEANS

The areas of ocean between the polar regions and the tropics are known as temperate, which means they have mild temperatures. Temperate seas cover parts of both hemispheres.

SAND HOPPER

On temperate seashores, when the Sun has set and the tide is low, it's safe for sand hoppers to come out and forage. These tiny crustaceans stay buried in the day, but have special 'compasses' in their brains and antennae to detect the Sun and Moon's movements.

HARBOUR PORPOISE

Harbour porpoises use **echolocation** to find their prey at night. They make fast clicking sounds which bounce off nearby objects, then use the returning echo to locate their victims. Some porpoises can catch ten fish in a single minute!

SCORPIONFISH

This scorpionfish has blotchy skin and a bumpy body to help it to blend in with the rocks on the ocean floor. Here it sits and waits to ambush its prey. It mostly hunts at night, when its camouflage is even more effective.

LOBSTER

Lobsters hide away during the day some rest in burrows, which they dig from the sand with their large front claws. At night, they crawl out to scavenge for food on the seabed.

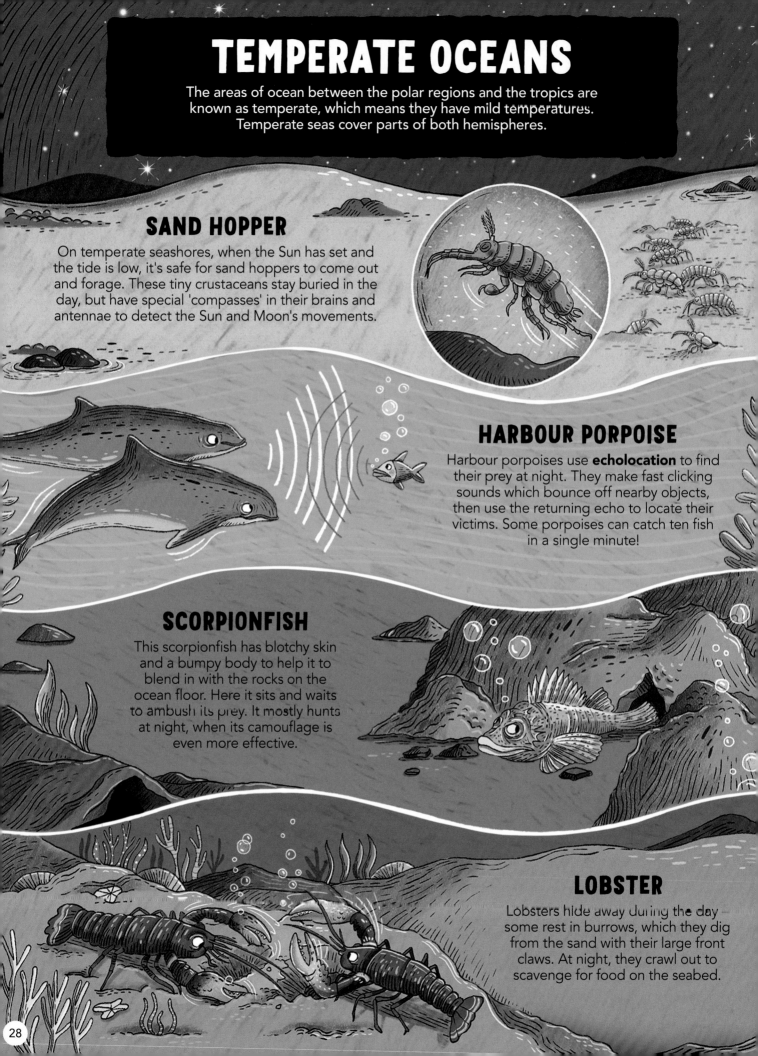

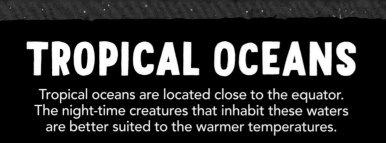

TROPICAL OCEANS

Tropical oceans are located close to the equator. The night-time creatures that inhabit these waters are better suited to the warmer temperatures.

HORSESHOE CRAB

This strange-looking horseshoe crab is older than the dinosaurs. Amazingly, the species has hardly changed in 445 million years. It has ten legs underneath its hard shell. It breeds at night, during a full or new Moon, when the high tides carry it up the beach to lay its eggs.

THE MOON AND TIDES

The Moon has a gravitational pull on the Earth's seas. This creates high and low tides. Some animals, such as horseshoe crabs, come ashore to lay their eggs during high tides – when seawater flows furthest up the beach – so they can reach the best places for their eggs to develop.

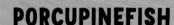

PORCUPINEFISH

The porcupinefish hunts for sea snails and crabs, which it then chews with its strong, beak-like jaws. It also has a spiky, defensive superpower: by quickly swallowing water, it can inflate like a prickly football, which few predators would want to go near.

MORAY EEL

This sharp-toothed eel hides under rocks until nightfall, when it can slither around without being seen. It's an ambush predator, lying in wait in the dark until its nostrils sense something close by.

TIGER MANTIS SHRIMP

In the darkness, this aggressive shrimp has special scales that detect pressure waves from passing fish. It's one of the ocean's fastest creatures, so when it strikes its prey, it can deliver a powerful punch at over 80 kilometres per hour (50 miles per hour).

LEATHERBACK SEA TURTLES

The origins of sea turtles stretch back more than 100 million years, to the age of the dinosaurs. These ancient reptiles spend most of their lives at sea – but their babies hatch on land, under cover of darkness.

Here in the Caribbean, a leatherback sea turtle is ready to lay her eggs. She arrives at night so she won't be disturbed.

During a full Moon, the ocean's high tides become even higher, meaning the sea travels further up the beach than usual. This makes it easier for the turtle to be carried up towards a spot which will stay dry.

When she finds a safe spot, she digs a hole in the sand. She lays her eggs – sometimes more than 100 – and then buries them to keep them hidden.

Having laid her eggs deep in the warm sand, this gentle giant returns to sea the same night. Her babies will hatch by themselves, many weeks from now.

Two months later, in the quiet of night, the nest stirs. Tiny beaks emerge out of the sand. At night, the air is cooler, and there are fewer birds and other predators around.

Birds such as the **caracara** are **diurnal**, so are only active in the day ...

... but **ghost crabs** hunt at night, so they are still a threat to baby turtles.

Each baby sea turtle is no bigger than the palm of your hand. Like their mother, they have a rounded shell, strong flippers and gleaming eyes.

Their first instinct is to head to the safety of the sea. While it's still dark, the hatchlings scuttle down to the water's edge.

When they reach the shoreline, the waves wash them into the ocean. For these babies, life at sea has begun.

Sadly, nearly all sea turtle species are endangered. Special areas are now being made to ensure turtles have safe, quiet and dark beaches where they can nest and hatch.

DO SEA CREATURES SLEEP?

Like humans, all marine animals need to rest in order to function and survive. Their sleeping habits, however, are very different from ours.

Some species of whale rest by either dangling down – like this peaceful pod of **sperm whales** – or floating like logs.

Some sea creatures, such as mackerel, tuna and some species of shark, have to keep moving 24 hours a day, even if their brains are resting. This is because in order to breathe, they need oxygenated water to be flowing over their gills at all times.

Some whales and dolphins keep moving while they snooze, shutting down one half of their brain while the other half stays awake. This helps them to stay alert to danger. After about two hours, they wake up the sleeping side of their brain then shut down the other half.

Jellyfish don't have brains, eyes or hearts but they still rest at night. **Cassiopea jellyfish** swim and rest upside down, pulsing 30 per cent less than they do in the day.

Some underwater animals rest by wedging themselves under rocks or into crevices. Others bob gently on the current.

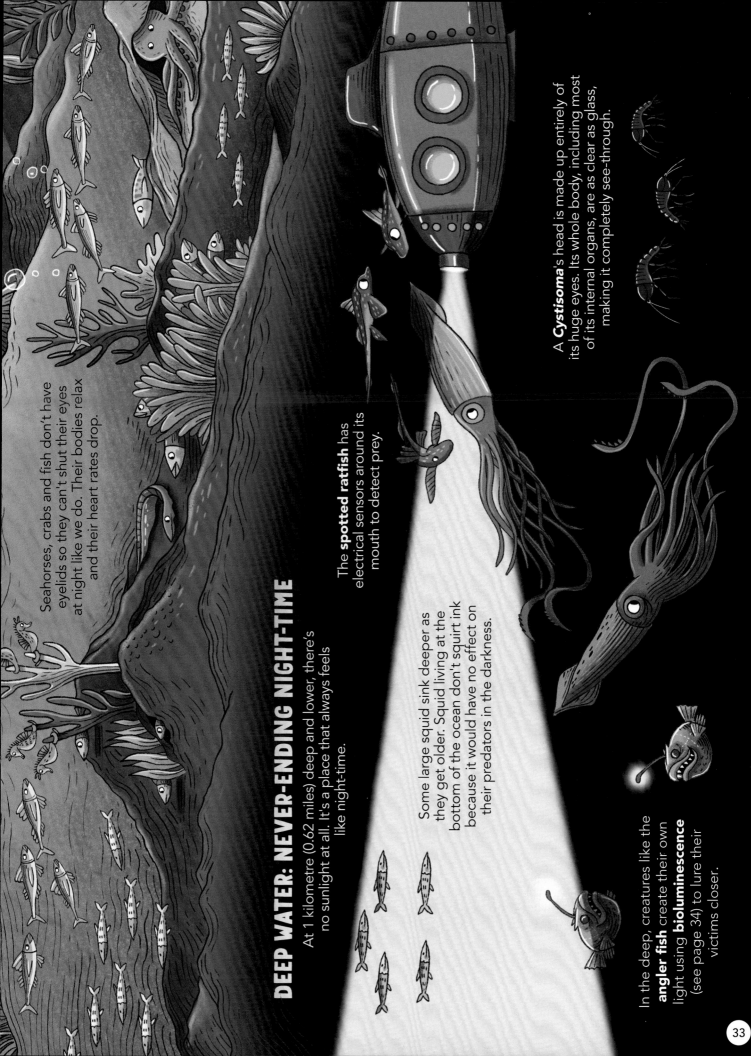

Seahorses, crabs and fish don't have eyelids so they can't shut their eyes at night like we do. Their bodies relax and their heart rates drop.

DEEP WATER: NEVER-ENDING NIGHT-TIME

At 1 kilometre (0.62 miles) deep and lower, there's no sunlight at all. It's a place that always feels like night-time.

The **spotted ratfish** has electrical sensors around its mouth to detect prey.

Some large squid sink deeper as they get older. Squid living at the bottom of the ocean don't squirt ink because it would have no effect on their predators in the darkness.

A **Cystisoma**'s head is made up entirely of its huge eyes. Its whole body, including most of its internal organs, are as clear as glass, making it completely see-through.

In the deep, creatures like the **angler fish** create their own light using **bioluminescence** (see page 34) to lure their victims closer.

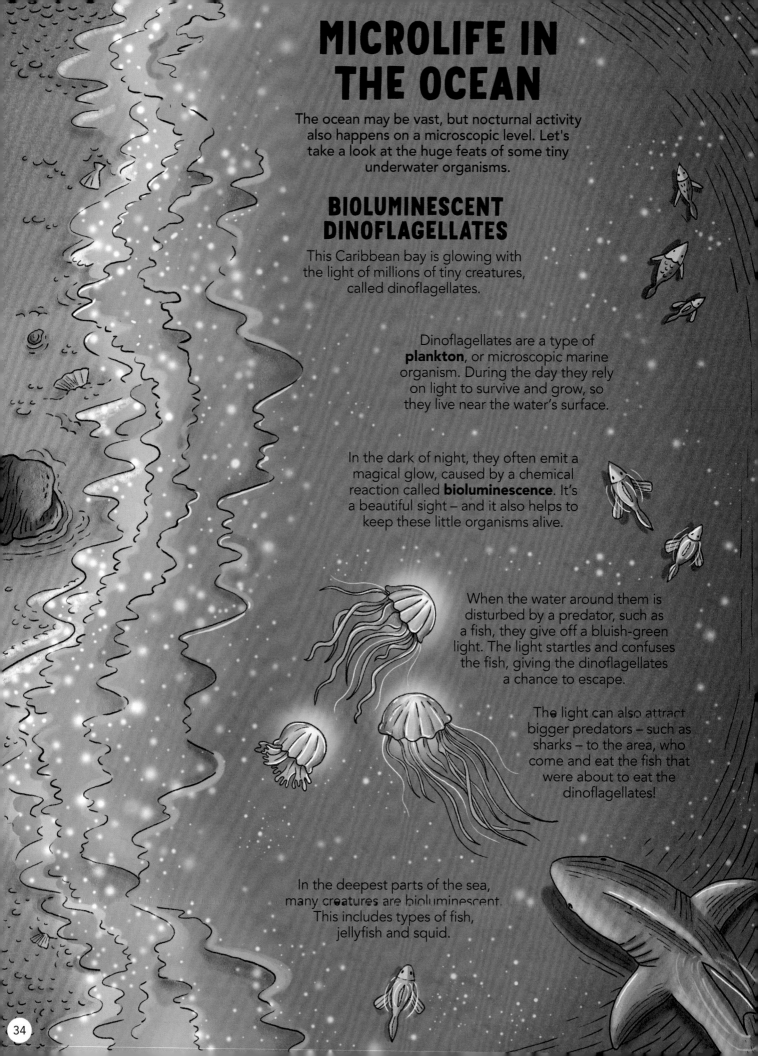

MICROLIFE IN THE OCEAN

The ocean may be vast, but nocturnal activity also happens on a microscopic level. Let's take a look at the huge feats of some tiny underwater organisms.

BIOLUMINESCENT DINOFLAGELLATES

This Caribbean bay is glowing with the light of millions of tiny creatures, called dinoflagellates.

Dinoflagellates are a type of **plankton**, or microscopic marine organism. During the day they rely on light to survive and grow, so they live near the water's surface.

In the dark of night, they often emit a magical glow, caused by a chemical reaction called **bioluminescence**. It's a beautiful sight – and it also helps to keep these little organisms alive.

When the water around them is disturbed by a predator, such as a fish, they give off a bluish-green light. The light startles and confuses the fish, giving the dinoflagellates a chance to escape.

The light can also attract bigger predators – such as sharks – to the area, who come and eat the fish that were about to eat the dinoflagellates!

In the deepest parts of the sea, many creatures are bioluminescent. This includes types of fish, jellyfish and squid.

DIEL VERTICAL MIGRATION

Every night of the year, billions of tiny fish and super-small sea creatures known as **zooplankton** swim up from the deepest, darkest parts of the ocean. This mass movement is called Diel Vertical Migration, and it's the largest animal migration on Earth.

In the daytime, the zooplankton hide in the depths of the sea, away from predators at the surface.

At night, when their predators are resting, it's safer for them to go to the surface, to feed and breed. Some travel upwards for more than 1 kilometre (0.62 miles) to reach the surface.

They usually swim downwards at sunrise, but during the long winters in the Arctic – when the Sun barely appears – they use the changes in moonlight to guide them. When the seasons change, and the nights get longer or shorter, their patterns shift to match.

In the morning, they sink back down to the bottom of the sea, to avoid being eaten by daytime predators. It's like a big game of hide-and-seek.

THE GREAT BARRIER REEF

This complex and colourful wonderland is the Great Barrier Reef, the planet's biggest coral reef system. It stretches for 2,300 kilometres (1,430 miles) along the east coast of Australia.

CORAL

A coral reef looks like a cluster of colourful rocks and plants, but it's actually made of lots of tiny, stony animals called **coral polyps**. Some are no bigger than a grain of sand.

After sundown they stretch out little tentacles to feed on the plankton that drift past at night.

Once a year, at night, something called **coral spawning** takes place. This is when each polyp releases a teeny bundle at the same time, filling the dark water with millions of specks. Some are polyp eggs.

Others are sperm, which makes the eggs fertile. When an egg bundle and a sperm bundle join together, they begin to create a new polyp.

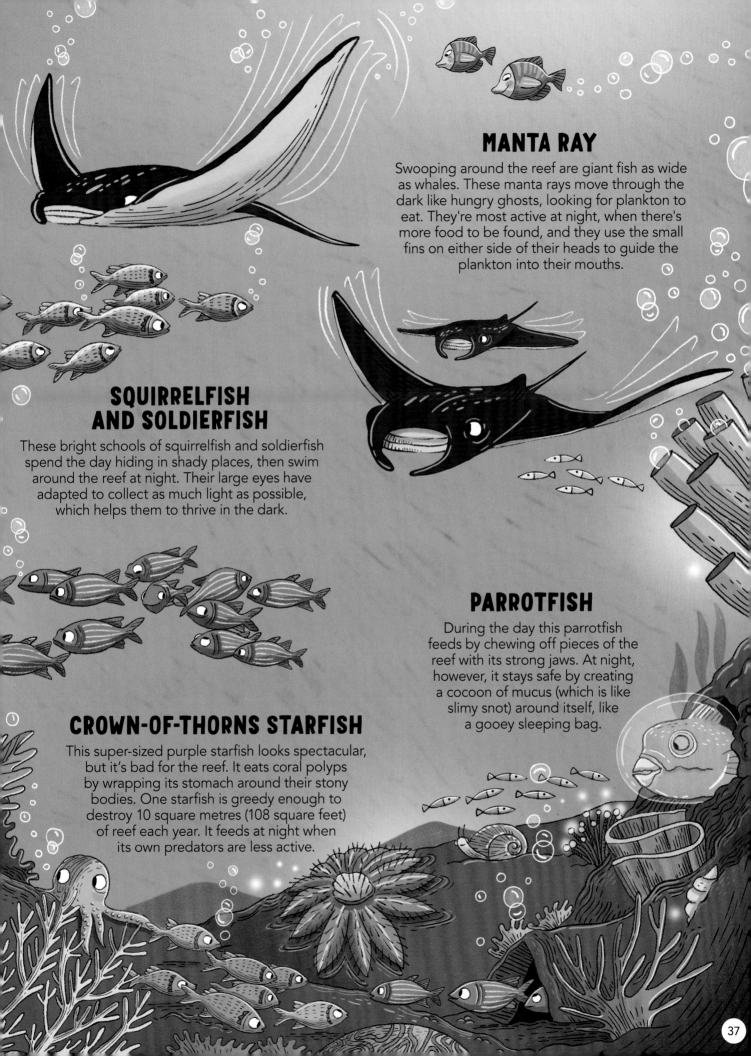

MANTA RAY

Swooping around the reef are giant fish as wide as whales. These manta rays move through the dark like hungry ghosts, looking for plankton to eat. They're most active at night, when there's more food to be found, and they use the small fins on either side of their heads to guide the plankton into their mouths.

SQUIRRELFISH AND SOLDIERFISH

These bright schools of squirrelfish and soldierfish spend the day hiding in shady places, then swim around the reef at night. Their large eyes have adapted to collect as much light as possible, which helps them to thrive in the dark.

PARROTFISH

During the day this parrotfish feeds by chewing off pieces of the reef with its strong jaws. At night, however, it stays safe by creating a cocoon of mucus (which is like slimy snot) around itself, like a gooey sleeping bag.

CROWN-OF-THORNS STARFISH

This super-sized purple starfish looks spectacular, but it's bad for the reef. It eats coral polyps by wrapping its stomach around their stony bodies. One starfish is greedy enough to destroy 10 square metres (108 square feet) of reef each year. It feeds at night when its own predators are less active.

FORESTS

It's the middle of the night in the forest. Leaves rustle, twigs snap, eyes flicker. Some animals are resting, but many are on the move, snuffling, creeping and doing what they can to feed and survive. Even the plants and trees have their own night-time habits. Darkness is here, but all over the world the woods are coming alive …

THE AMAZON RAINFOREST

The sound of buzzing insects and croaking frogs fills the warm, humid night. Hungry creatures prowl through the dark. Tropical rainforests are found all over the world. The Amazon rainforest, in South America, is the world's largest.

This **kinkajou** is a small tropical mammal that spends the day sleeping in hollow tree trunks, then comes out at night to feed. The bottoms of its paws are bare-skinned to help it to feel its way along branches in the dark. Its hearing is so sharp that it can even tell when a snake is nearby.

Sometimes nicknamed the 'owl monkey' for its big eyes, the **night monkey** is the only monkey in the world that is truly nocturnal. It becomes more active when the Moon is bright as it can see its surroundings even more clearly.

Blinking on and off like tiny golden sparks, these **fireflies** twinkle in the dark. The insects can control when they flash, thanks to a clever chemical reaction inside their bodies. They do it as a warning to predators, and to attract mating partners.

With petals shining bright, this is a type of cactus called an **Amazon moonflower.** Each of its flowers blooms for a single night, opening after sunset and dying before sunrise. The flower sends a special scent into the night air to attract a nocturnal pollinator: the **hawkmoth.** After feeding on the flower's nectar, the moth carries grains of pollen to another flower. Other night-blooming plants in the Amazon are pollinated by bats.

Here's the ultimate jungle hunter. This **jaguar** can cover more than 10 kilometres (6.21 miles) in a single night, stalking the rainforest in search of a meal. Its paws are padded with soft tissue, which help it to move quietly along the forest floor. Its coat is covered with jagged black spots – called rosettes – which help it to blend into the dark, patchy shadows of the rainforest.

This shy **tapir** is the largest land mammal in the Amazon. At night, it forages on plants and bananas. It uses its long, powerful nose to locate food, and to detect and avoid predators.

WILD BEARDED PIGS

In the rainforests of Borneo, in Southeast Asia, creepers hang from the trees and strange noises echo through the jungle. It's night-time, and an army of snuffling herbivores is on the move.

Bearded pigs are usually active during the day, foraging for food with their long noses or wallowing in mud baths. Tonight, however, they're on an important nocturnal mission.

This bushy-bearded herd is starting a migration that will cover hundreds of kilometres. It will take them several weeks or months, and they will do it only at night.

The pigs' migration is believed to be triggered by **dipterocarp trees** producing bumper crops of fruit and nuts (called **masting**). When the trees mast, the pigs move as a group to bulk up on the oil-rich seeds.

The older males, who know the route well, lead the herd through the dark forest, patiently heading onwards. Walking in the darkness has risks, but it's still safer for them than in the bright daylight.

GLOW-IN-THE-DARK MUSHROOMS

These wild tropical fungi look normal in the daylight, but at night they shine like green fairy lanterns. They release a chemical compound called **luciferin**, which produces light when mixed with oxygen. Their glow attracts insects, who then help to spread mushroom spores (a bit like seeds) to other parts of the forest.

It's several weeks later, and the herd meets an obstacle: a wide river. Together, the pigs plough into the water, using their powerful legs to swim to the other bank, then continue on their way. They are also capable of swimming between islands.

The herd is nearing the end of its journey, but not before one last challenge. The path steepens as the pigs begin to climb a mountain. Thankfully, they are as good at climbing as they are swimming. The forested mountainside keeps them relatively hidden, though they never know when a predator might be watching.

CLOUDED LEOPARD

This secretive cat is a clouded leopard. It's an excellent climber and likes hiding in the darkness of the branches, where it waits to pounce on young bearded pigs and other creatures that pass below. It prefers hunting at night, when there are fewer animals competing for the same prey.

Finally, these determined animals arrive at their destination. It's been many months, and their reward is welcome: a feast of fruit and nuts, which will help them to stay strong and breed more piglets. This herd's nocturnal trek is over – for now, at least.

EUROPEAN FORESTS

The forests of western Europe are very different to the jungles of the tropics. At night they're colder, and at first, they seem quieter. But if you step among the oak and holly trees, you'll find plenty of life stirring …

PLANTS AT NIGHT

All around the world, trees and plants stay busy even after dark. During the day, they perform something called **photosynthesis**, using the energy in sunlight to turn water and a gas – called carbon dioxide – into food for themselves. At the same time, they release oxygen (the gas that humans and animals breathe) into the air.

Photosynthesis stops at night, but plants keep working. Even though they don't have lungs, plants are 'breathing' 24 hours a day, taking in small amounts of oxygen and releasing carbon dioxide. This is called **respiration** and it helps to keep a natural balance of gases in the air and soil.

Plants don't just breathe at night; they also keep growing, using the energy they stored during the day.

On the edge of the woods live strange beetles called **glow-worms**. They are similar to the fireflies of the Amazon. On a summer night, female glow-worms can make their bottoms shine green, to attract male glow-worms. Without wings, the females often climb to the top of tall grass stems, to make sure their glowing backsides can be seen!

When the Sun goes down, **bats** appear. These fast-flying mammals live their lives in almost constant darkness. Their eyes are tiny, so they hunt using an amazing method called **echolocation**.

They do this by making lots of little clicking or whistling sounds. The sounds return to the bats' ears by bouncing back off insects, leaves or whatever else is nearby. This makes a 'picture' for the bats in the dark, telling them where to fly to gobble up midges and moths!

Watch out for this quiet killer – the **tawny owl**. It has soft edges to its feathered wings, so it can fly without making a sound. It likes to perch on high branches, using its excellent hearing and eyesight to detect mice and voles on the forest floor. When it spots food, the owl swoops down to catch its prey with its sharp claws, called **talons**.

Badgers don't often see the daylight. They spend their days in deep, pitch-black burrows called **setts**, coming out after sunset to root around for worms and insects. Like many animals living underground, badgers have small eyes that won't get grit or soil in them. Instead, they have powerful paws and sensitive noses to find food above ground in the darkness.

HOW DO ANIMALS SEE AT NIGHT?

At night, human eyes can't see very well. The shapes and details are dim and fuzzy. But for many nocturnal animals, the world looks just as clear at night as it does to us humans in the daytime.

BIGGER EYES

Many nocturnal animals have bigger eyes for their body size compared to daytime animals.

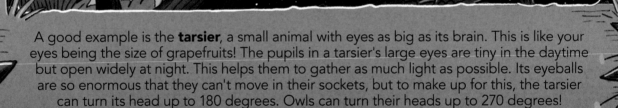

A good example is the **tarsier**, a small animal with eyes as big as its brain. This is like your eyes being the size of grapefruits! The pupils in a tarsier's large eyes are tiny in the daytime but open widely at night. This helps them to gather as much light as possible. Its eyeballs are so enormous that they can't move in their sockets, but to make up for this, the tarsier can turn its head up to 180 degrees. Owls can turn their heads up to 270 degrees!

Tree frogs have good night vision thanks to their bulging eyes, which allow them to see not only in front, but also to the sides and slightly behind them.

A **gecko**'s eyes are 350 times more sensitive than human eyes. This means that, even in low light, they can make out different colours.

RODS AND CONES

Inside every eyeball is a **retina** – a thin layer that detects light using special cells, called **rods** and **cones**. Rods sense shape and movement and work well even when there is not much light. Cones can sense colours and detail, but they work best in bright light.

Nocturnal animals often have many more rods than cones, which makes them extremely good at seeing in the dark. Owls, for example, have very large retinas, packed with up to five times more rods than humans. Most owls, however, cannot see many colours – they see the world in black, white and shades of grey.

RETINA

INSIDE AN OWL'S EYE

TAPETUM LUCIDUM

Lots of nocturnal creatures have a tapetum lucidum – a layer of tissue behind the retina. It acts like a mirror. Light coming into the eye reflects off the tapetum lucidum and back into the retina. Because the retina receives the same light twice, this improves night vision.

When an animal's eyes shine brightly in the light of a torch or car headlamp, this is because of the tapetum lucidum.

Other animals have different ways of 'seeing' in the dark. In Central America, there's a snake that dangles from cave ceilings. It uses **infrared sensitivity** to find its prey. This means it can sense the body heat given off by bats flying past. One snap, and they're caught!

PLAINS AND DESERTS

It's two hours after sunset on the African savannah. The sky is full of stars and a soft breeze blows through the acacia trees. You might expect it to be quiet, but on plains and deserts around the world, creatures of all shapes and sizes are starting to stir. Away from the scorching heat and exposing glare of the daytime, the dark brings animals a chance to travel, hide, graze and hunt.

THE SAVANNAH

On the grasslands of the African savannah, wide, thorny trees dot the earth and darkness cloaks the hills – but everywhere you turn, animals are watching, creeping and stalking.

A **South African bushbaby** has huge eyes to see in the dark, and large ears for hearing insects moving through the branches. They look cute, but bushbabies have a strange habit – they often wee on their hands and feet! This might be to help them to grip tree branches tightly.

This scruffy **brown hyena** has special sensory powers. It uses its incredible sense of smell to locate a night-time meal, walking up to 40 kilometres (24.9 miles) a night. Its nose has many more olfactory receptors, or smell detectors, than human noses do. This helps it to pick up the scent of 'carrion' – animals that other creatures have killed – more than 1 kilometre (0.62 miles) away.

This **crested porcupine** spends the night foraging for roots, plant bulbs and fruit. If predators get too close it fans out its quills and shakes its backside, rattling its spikes in the darkness.

These pale flowers belong to a plant called a **night phlox**. It opens its star-like petals after sunset, releasing a sweet honey smell into the air. This helps it to attract moths and other nocturnal insects, which can spread its pollen.

Lots of African insects are active in the daytime, but **armoured bush crickets** appear at night – and they're loud! Male crickets scrape their wings together, making a screeching sound that echoes through the darkness. This deafening noise scares off predators, warning them not to come closer, but it attracts female crickets.

Hippos spend the day wallowing in muddy water to keep cool. The Sun is often too hot for them, but when the temperature has dropped at night, they waddle on to the riverbanks to chomp on the grass. They can sleep both in water and on land.

This **mongoose** is shy and nocturnal, and has a long white tail to trick its predators. If a white-tailed mongoose is hunted in the dark, its attacker is more likely to pounce on its tail, rather than the darker head and body.

AFRICAN LIONS

A pride of lions is a sight to fear. Their teeth are sharp, their claws are strong and their golden coats blend in with the tawny grass. Female lions do almost all of the hunting, and 90 per cent of their kills happen at night.

It's early evening on the African savannah. As the light fades, the lionesses break away from the pride and begin travelling over the grasslands, looking for prey.

They sometimes stalk the plains during the day, but they often choose to start hunting in the murky twilight, when it's easier for them to stay hidden. Animals that are active at dawn and dusk can be described as **crepuscular**.

As darkness descends, the lionesses' night vision kicks in. The pale markings underneath their eyes also help to reflect light back into their pupils.

The lionesses often hunt in groups of two or three. Antelopes and zebras may not have the best eyesight but they can run fast, so the lionesses must work together if they want to catch a meal.

Lionesses find it harder to catch prey on bright moonlit nights – it's easier for them to hunt under the cover of total darkness. Tonight it's a new Moon – the perfect conditions for staying hidden.

In the distance, a lone impala appears, grazing the long grass. The lionesses know this is their chance for a kill.

They hunker down and creep forwards, approaching the young antelope quietly and carefully.

When they get close, they wait … then they pounce!

The impala tries to run, but it's no match for the strength and teamwork of the lionesses. Tonight, the pride will eat well.

Lionesses aren't always this successful at hunting. In general, less than a quarter of their attempts end with a kill.

NIGHT HUNTERS ON PLAINS

Dingoes are a type of Australian wild dog. In the hottest parts of the country, they often hunt in the cool of the night. They use their flexible paw joints to help them to climb in search of food.

Pumas, also called mountain lions or cougars, live in North and South America. They hunt alone, and of all the cats have the largest hind legs for their size. They can take on prey three times their weight, such as vicuña.

DESERT TEMPERATURES

During the day, deserts are the hottest places on the planet. But at night, something unexpected happens – the temperatures take a huge nosedive.

Death Valley, in California, is the driest and hottest place in North America. Its daytime temperatures have reached as high as 56.7 degrees Celsius (134 degrees Fahrenheit) – few animals and plants can survive in such exteme heat.

The valley is surrounded by four mountain ranges. The fierce heat from the Sun is reflected off the dunes, then trapped by the surrounding mountains. But at night, the thermometer can drop to a freezing –4 degrees Celcius (25 degrees Fahrenheit).

WHY ARE DESERTS SO COLD AT NIGHT?

The first reason is the sand. Unlike soil, it's not very good at storing heat. Sand only stays hot when the Sun is heating it up. So when the Sun disappears, the warmth in the sand vanishes into the night.

The second reason Is the dry air. There's almost no humidity (wetness) in the desert air. In a rainforest, the humidity in the moist air keeps the land warm – a bit like a giant blanket. But in the desert, the dry air isn't able to hold on to the heat.

HOW IS DESERT WILDLIFE ADAPTED TO THE COLD?

Here in the Sonoran Desert, in North America, the **Desert Ironwood tree** acts as a 'nurse plant', keeping the saplings and seedlings below it warmer at night.

The pretty **Costa's hummingbird** slows its heart rate down at night, from more than 500 beats a minute to just 50 beats a minute. This helps the bird to use its energy to keep warm instead.

Pronghorn antelopes have hollow hairs that trap body heat. This helps them to stay warmer when the temperature drops.

Just as humans can stay warm by exercising, **moths** can increase their body heat by whirring their wings.

Moths pollinate the night-blooming **cereus**, a type of cactus that flowers in the dark.

THE ARABIAN DESERT

Let's journey to the soft, rolling sand dunes of the
Arabian Desert. The animals that appear here at night
are well adapted to the dry, chilly conditions.

Stalking stealthily through the moonlight
comes a **sand cat**. Its large ears are set low –
lower than a domestic cat – listening out
for the squeaks of its prey on the ground.
The cat's fur keeps it warm in the
cold night air.

Looking like a cross between a mouse and a
kangaroo, this cute little rodent is a **jerboa**. Its
whiskers help it to get a sense of its surroundings,
both in its burrow and out in the night air, and its
bat-like ears listen out for danger nearby.

Both animals have furry feet, which protect them
from the hot sand in the day, and help to keep
them warm at night. The fur grips the sand when
they run or change direction, stopping them from
slipping. Their footprints are hard to track, as the
cushioning stops their paws from sinking
too far into the sand.

The animal under these huge ears is a **fennec fox**. Its hearing is so good that it can track down insects under the sand, but its ears have another job, too. Because the blood vessels in each ear are so close to the skin's surface, they release body heat during the day, keeping the fox cool for its night-time hunting.

In colder parts of the world, snakes are active in the daytime, but this **horned viper** comes out at night, when the desert heat has died down. It lies in wait to ambush lizards and sometimes even hedgehogs. Its sand-coloured body blends with its surroundings and makes it even harder to spot in the dark.

The **desert hedgehog** is a fearless and prickly character. Faced with a horned viper, the hedgehog can use its sharp spines for protection, and its jaws are strong enough to bite through the reptile's neck. A desert hedgehog's kidneys are specially adapted to conserve water – a big help in an environment with so little moisture.

If you hear a strange, repeating note of birdsong in the starlit desert, it's probably a **nightjar**. This special bird stays camouflaged in the day, then feeds on insects at night. Its beak is very wide, helping it to catch bugs as it flies over the sand.

THE ENDS OF THE EARTH

Winter nights in the polar regions are starlit, freezing and very, very long. In both the Arctic and Antarctica – at the top and bottom of the world – the lands and seas are plunged into darkness for weeks, or even months, at a time. With icy plains stretching as far as the eye can see, humans and animals in these regions have to be tough and smart to survive.

POLAR NIGHTS

In Arctic regions, night-time can last for several months. These long stretches of darkness are called polar nights, and for the animals living here, they present many challenges and opportunities.

WHAT ARE POLAR NIGHTS?

Polar nights are caused by the Earth's tilt on its axis – in the winter, the northernmost areas of the planet are angled away from the Sun. As the Earth turns, the Arctic is blocked from the Sun's rays, in some areas for months on end.

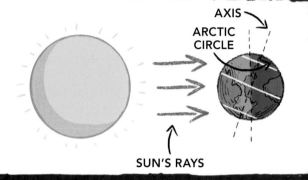

AXIS

ARCTIC CIRCLE

SUN'S RAYS

The closer you are to the North Pole, the longer the polar night is. In areas where the Sun sits just below the horizon, the sky is a midnight blue.

The prolonged darkness brings harsh conditions. Its residents have to adapt to the brutal, freezing temperatures.

In Kangerlussuaq, in Greenland, some winter nights last 22 hours. For extra insulation against the cold, **musk oxen** grow a second coat, which they shed at the end of winter.

Banks Island, in Canada, has almost three months a year with no daylight. **Arctic hares** here have short legs, ears and tails to help them to retain as much heat as possible.

Svalbard, in Norway, is also in almost total darkness for three months of the year. The **Svalbard reindeer** is stockier than other reindeer species, to cope with the cold.

WINTER IN ALASKA

Here in Alaska, winter is closing in and animals are preparing for the dark nights ahead.

Some animals, such as **caribou**, migrate. Others, like these **Arctic ground squirrels**, hibernate.

For others, life here goes on. **Arctic wolves** hunt by the moonlight, using their sense of smell to pinpoint prey from over 2 kilometres (1.24 miles) away.

Arctic foxes also hunt through the long polar night. Their sensitive ears detect the high-pitched sounds of prey scurrying beneath the snow.

The **great horned owl** has special eye cells that give it excellent night vision. Its fringed wing feathers help it to glide silently towards its prey.

THE NORTHERN LIGHTS

On clear winter nights in the Arctic, the skies fill with waves of rainbow-coloured light that swirl and dance in the dark. This breathtaking spectacle is called the **aurora borealis**, or the Northern Lights.

WHAT CAUSES THE NORTHERN LIGHTS?

The lights appear due to 'storms' or the Sun, millions of kilometres away. During a solar storm, the surface of the Sun flares up, sending out clouds of little particles. When the particles approach Earth, they're attracted to the North and South Poles, where the world's magnetic field is strongest. As they get closer, they mingle with gases in our atmosphere, which makes them glow.

The Northern Lights happen throughout the year, but it's in the dark of the winter night that they can be seen most brightly. The lights can be green, pink, blue, orange, violet or yellow.

The same thing happens in the winter skies at the other end of the world, down in Antarctica. There we call it the **aurora australis**, or the Southern Lights.

You might think living here during the polar nights would be unbearable without the warmth and light of the Sun. But many people here embrace it – getting outside to ski, hike and dog-sled beneath the beautiful sky. People also enjoy the peacefulness and coziness of the season, lighting candles and gathering around burning woodstoves. Many also use special lamps inside which mimic sunlight.

People in the Arctic region have been fascinated by the Northern Lights for thousands of years. Some used to believe that the lights were a sign from their gods or spirit ancestors. In Finland, the name for the Northern Lights is *revontulet*, meaning 'fox fires'. According to myth, foxes made of fire once lived in Lapland and created sparks in the sky with their tails.

ANTARCTICA

At the bottom of the world, in Antarctica, scientists and researchers come to learn more about this huge, empty continent. Nearly 5,000 scientists live and study here in the summer, and around 1,000 of them remain here during the polar night in winter.

The polar night becomes longer the closer you are to the South Pole. Scientists have to live carefully in the long, dark winter. Very few planes or boats can reach them at this time of year, so they have to stay here until the polar night has ended.

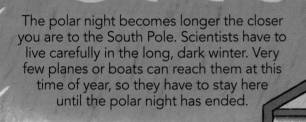

If the scientists spend time outside, they need special clothes to stay safe in the dark. To survive the coldest nights on Earth, they have to wear long thermal underwear, lots of warm layers, windproof jackets, insulated boots, thick gloves and hats or balaclavas.

When they need to move from one building to another, they often have ropes to hold on to. The ropes are important during blizzards, when the night is full of whirling snow.

Whereas the North Pole sits in the middle of the frozen sea, the South Pole is on land covered by thick ice, making it higher above sea level. This means the polar nights here are even colder, drier and windier than in the Arctic.

Antarctica offers the clearest view of space from Earth.

The scientists spend most of their time in bases called research stations, where they can eat, work and sleep. The stations have very thick, strong walls and are built on raised platforms – if they were built into the ground, the snow would bury them. By raising them up, the snow can pass underneath instead.

WHERE ARE THE ANIMALS?

Because of the bitter temperatures and the fierce winds, very few creatures can survive the months of darkness. Some seals, whales and seabirds stay in the region all year, but many travel north before the polar night arrives. Several species of penguins live in or around Antarctica, but most of them leave, too, to avoid the extreme cold.

EMPEROR PENGUINS

As the long polar night approaches, thousands of
emperor penguins in Antarctica are preparing
for an important job ...

Most animals escape Antarctica at this time of
year, by swimming or flying across the seas. But
as winter approaches, the emperor penguins
march inland instead, away from the coast.

After making the long walk to
their **rookery** – the place where
they can raise their chicks – the
penguins start to breed.

The females lay one egg each. The males
look after the eggs – just as the polar night
really begins. For two whole months, the male
penguins huddle together in the freezing night,
keeping their eggs safe in a pouch between
their feet. During this time, these devoted
dads live in darkness – and have no food!

The females, meanwhile,
return to the sea, spending
many weeks fattening up
on fish. This helps them
to restore their energy
and grow strong enough
to feed up the chick
when it arrives.

Emperor penguins are the largest and heaviest of all the penguin species. They have chunky bodies and two layers of feathers, all of which help them to stay strong and warm in the dark winter.

Even with snowstorms blowing, and the temperatures dropping to −40 degrees Celsius (−40 degrees Fahrenheit), the colony of males stays where it is.

The penguins take it in turns to shuffle to the centre of the huddle, where it's warmer and more sheltered. By working together as a team, they can survive the harsh conditions of the polar night.

After more than eight weeks, as the polar night starts to fade and the skies become lighter, the eggs finally hatch. Each one reveals a grey, fluffy chick.

Soon afterwards, the female penguins return to the colony.

They feed the chick by coughing up a sticky, fishy mixture from their stomachs. It's yucky for us, but tasty for a penguin chick!

And so family life begins – until the next polar night, when it's time to start all over again …

67

ANIMALS IN CITIES

We usually think of cities as human places, but at night many of them are crawling with wildlife. As cities around the globe become bigger, and the countryside becomes smaller, some animals have no choice but to learn to survive on the streets. A city might seem like an overwhelming place for an animal, but it offers many of the same opportunities that it does for humans – the chance to find food, shelter and family. So every evening, surrounded by concrete towers and electric lights, creatures large and small move through the urban night.

LONDON, UK

Red foxes have been spotted in London for about 100 years, and they usually explore at night. Foxes more commonly live in the countryside, but because humans have disturbed their territories, many have been forced to survive in the city and adapt to a different way of life.

In the city it's safer for the foxes after dark, because there are fewer people around to disturb them, and fewer cars and buses to avoid on the roads. City nights also offer lots of leftover food that's been thrown away, making it easier to find a meal here than in the countryside.

Foxes move quickly and quietly, following their noses to find food. They're not fussy eaters: vegetable scraps and old chicken bones from a bin can provide the perfect dinner. They're also good at hunting urban rats and pigeons.

ROBINS

It's not unusual to hear robins singing in the middle of the night in London, even though they're diurnal. There are so many streetlights here that some birds get confused and treat it like daytime.

TOKYO, JAPAN

When the Sun goes down, Tokyo becomes a neon jungle. As the streets crackle with bright lights, insects and reptiles stir to life.

Cicadas spend the first years of their lives underground, feeding on nutrients from the roots of trees and getting stronger.

Once a cicada is old enough to mate, it emerges from its burrow in the heart of the city. It comes out at night, when there are fewer predatory birds around. It climbs a tree, attaches itself to a branch and sheds its skin, becoming a winged adult.

The males then use a loud, high-pitched mating call to attract females. Here in Tokyo, the sound echoes off the tall buildings, making the call even easier to hear.

GECKOS

Cities like Tokyo are also a good habitat for geckos – small lizards that can walk up walls and across ceilings, using their sticky foot pads. At night, they often wait near electric lights, which attract tasty flies and spiders.

CITY NIGHTS

What else is scurrying through city streets at night? Let's take a look at other urban wildlife around the world.

Hundreds of years ago, the area that is now New York City was cloaked in forest. **Raccoons** lived there then – and they're still a common sight in New York today. These nocturnal creatures have adapted brilliantly to life in the city, climbing fire escapes to find shelter and rummaging through restaurant bins for food.

On the outskirts of the Indian city of Mumbai, **leopards** slink through the streets by moonlight. The spotted cats stay in the wild on the outskirts of the city during the day, but at night they can find prey in the suburbs. The leopards hunt stray dogs and wild pigs, which they know can be found by rubbish bins outside factories and apartments, looking for their own food.

The German capital city of Berlin has lots of big wooded parks. Herds of **wild boar** live here, and snuffle out on to the streets after dark. Their eyesight is poor but their sense of smell is excellent, so they have no trouble sniffing out food. They gobble up almost anything, from rotten eggs to old sandwiches.

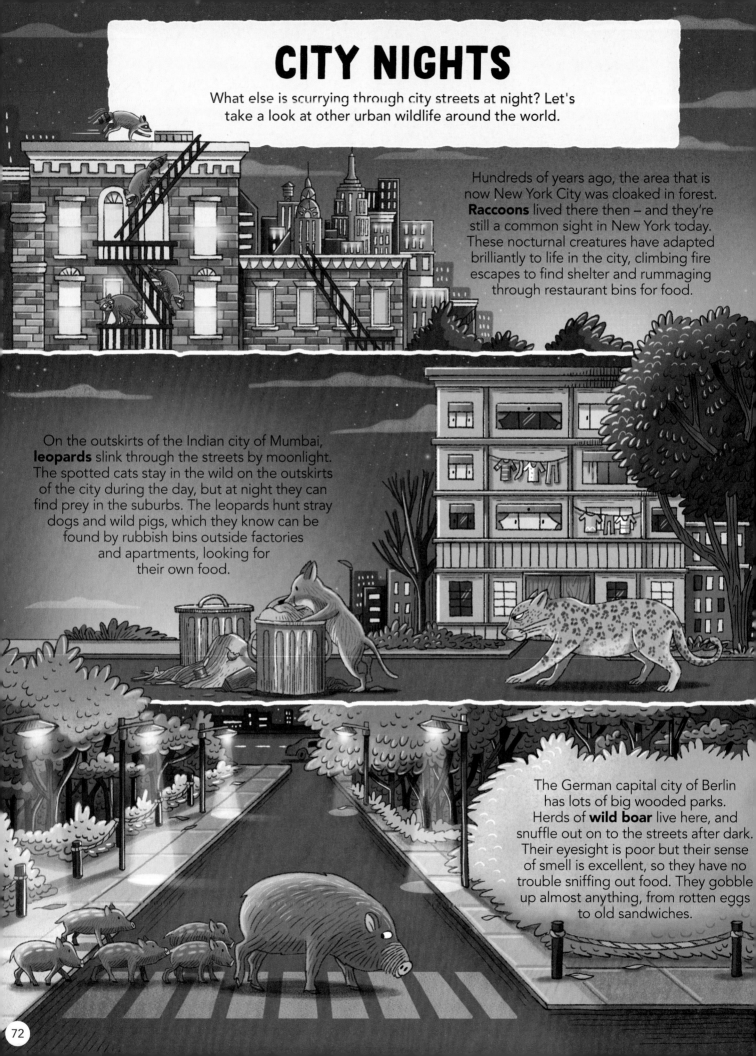

If you see a wide pair of wings soaring through the dark in Sydney, Australia, they might belong to a species called the **powerful owl**. These huge owls usually hunt in the countryside, but they've learned that the city suburbs hold lots of food for them. **Possums** live here in high numbers, and the owls love eating them.

In Mexico City, **cacomistles** tiptoe through people's gardens. They feed on everything from fruit and insects to small reptiles, all of which can be found near houses. These rare, shy, raccoon-like creatures spend most of their lives in trees, so cities with green spaces – where they can nip up and down trunks and branches at night – suit them well.

The South African city of Cape Town has some unusual wildlife, including a wild cat called the **caracal**. Often spotted on Table Mountain, which overlooks the city, these stealthy cats have also been seen creeping into urban areas, in search of juicy prey such as rats or guinea fowl.

BROWN RATS

Rats are better adapted to urban life than any other wild mammal. Almost every city in the world has a large population of them living in sewers, buildings and gardens. Here in the busy city of Chicago, USA, rats have made themselves at home.

Rats are often unpopular with people because they carry disease and spread germs. But they're also very clever – and by mainly appearing at night for food, they thrive as a species.

During the day, this colony of brown rats stays safe in the sewers below ground. Rats can also live under floorboards, between walls, in dark roof spaces and even on ships – which is how they first spread to cities across the world.

Now that night-time has arrived, the rats use their long, sharp claws to easily scale the walls of the sewer.

They reach a complex maze of pipes, where their excellent hearing and sense of smell help them to find their way to the surface. Each rat has up to 70 long, sensitive whiskers, which it uses to feel its surroundings.

They reach ground level, flattening their ribcages to squeeze through the sewer grate, then start sniffing for food. Rats have lived near humans for thousands of years. They're smart enough to know that where there are people, there's also food waste.

Rats have weak eyesight, but streetlights help them to see where they're going. They pitter-patter towards the bins, their dark fur keeping them hidden while they're out in the open.

Dinner time begins. Rats eat everything from leftover pizza and meat scraps to mouldy fruit peel and old pet food – they're not picky!

The easy supply of night-time food is only one reason why there are so many rats in our cities. It's also because they breed so often. Amazingly, a colony of urban rats can grow from less than ten to almost 12,000 in a single year!

HUMANS

More than eight billion humans live on Earth. No matter who we are, we all experience night and day, and we all need regular sleep. Right now, as you're reading this, at least one billion people are fast asleep. But night isn't a time of rest for everyone. With so many people working or having fun under the glow of electric lights, human activity keeps going right around the clock.

SLEEP AND DREAMS

For humans and for most of the animal kingdom, good sleep is key to survival. It helps us to rest and recover our brains and bodies so that they can function properly the next day.

SLEEP CYCLES

When we sleep at night, we usually go through four or five sleep cycles, each lasting up to two hours. One sleep cycle is made up of four sleep stages.

Stage One is short. This is when we drift off and go from being awake to being asleep.

Stage Two is when our minds and muscles really start to relax. In these first two stages, it's easiest for us to be woken up.

Stage Three is known as deep sleep. When we enter deep sleep, our bodies and brains slow down even further.

Stage Four is known as Rapid Eye Movement sleep, or REM sleep. Our eyes flicker around under our eyelids and our minds become busier. This is when most dreams happen.

CIRCADIAN RHYTHM

Almost all living things, including humans, follow a natural 24-hour pattern called a circadian rhythm. This is part of our inner body clock, and it tells us when to sleep and when to wake. If our normal sleep routine is interrupted, for example by bright lights or a very late night, this can confuse our circadian rhythm.

WHAT ARE DREAMS?

Even when we're asleep, our brains stay active. We're not making decisions or coming up with ideas, but our resting minds are still busy. Our imaginations create pictures and situations that become dreams.

Some scientists think that when we see things in our dreams, it could be our way of solving problems, or sorting through our memories. When we dream, our brains replay events from the day, and mix them with other – sometimes unrelated – experiences. In doing this, our brains are sifting through what's important to hold on to and what's not, and helping us to remember new information.

Often, we dream about people we know well, or things that we're nervous or excited about. At other times, our dreams are just very strange! Our most vivid dreams happen during the REM stage of the sleep cycle. We usually have four to six dreams a night, but most of us only remember one or two every week.

Experts think that many animals dream, including mammals, birds and maybe even spiders! Perhaps you've noticed a pet cat or dog twitching while they doze. Some dogs give muffled barks when they're fast asleep. Scientists are discovering similar behaviours in other animals – such as octopuses, which have been shown to display bursts of arm and eye movements while asleep, and even change the patterns on their skin.

WHERE HUMANS SLEEP

Most of us spend the night in our beds, in our bedrooms. But some of us sleep in very interesting places!

On the International Space Station, astronauts spend the night in sleeping bags strapped to the walls, to stop themselves floating around.

Rock climbers sometimes sleep on special platforms called 'portaledges', which attach to the sides of cliffs. They're like hanging beds!

Every night, there are people asleep on boats, planes and trains. On some overnight trains, the bunk beds are three beds high.

Some long-distance trucks have a special bed behind the seats. The drivers can spend the night resting here, before continuing again in the morning.

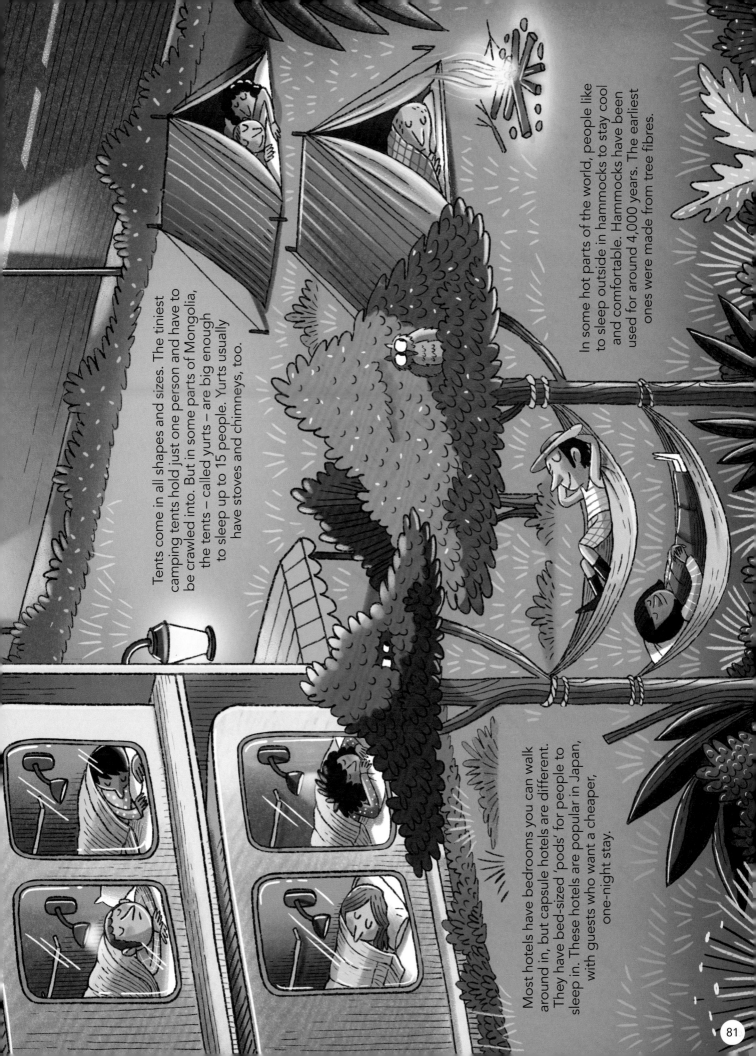

Tents come in all shapes and sizes. The tiniest camping tents hold just one person and have to be crawled into. But in some parts of Mongolia, the tents – called yurts – are big enough to sleep up to 15 people. Yurts usually have stoves and chimneys, too.

In some hot parts of the world, people like to sleep outside in hammocks to stay cool and comfortable. Hammocks have been used for around 4,000 years. The earliest ones were made from tree fibres.

Most hotels have bedrooms you can walk around in, but capsule hotels are different. They have bed-sized 'pods' for people to sleep in. These hotels are popular in Japan, with guests who want a cheaper, one-night stay.

ELECTRIC LIGHT

If you looked at the Earth at night from space, you'd see parts of the world lit up like fairy lights. Amazingly, this glow is 100 per cent human-made, caused by electric light. After dark, our busiest towns and cities spark to life.

Just a few hundred years ago, the same view would have been much darker. Before electric lights became common, humans used candles, oil lamps and gas lights. Going back further, our ancestors had to rely on fires for light and warmth. These fires wouldn't have been visible from space.

Humans first harnessed electricity in the 19th century, and it changed the way we experience night. These days, when evening comes, the Sun's rays are replaced by the glow of streetlamps and the bright lights of restaurants, hotels and late-night shops.

In hot countries, football and other sports are often played at night, under floodlights. Some matches don't kick off until 9PM – and at some tennis tournaments, the players are still going well after midnight!

MARACANÃ STADIUM, BRAZIL

Plays, musicals and operas are often held late in the evening, too, so that people can enjoy them once their own jobs have finished. Brightly lit fast-food outlets and petrol stations are also still open into the early hours, and hospitals stay open 24/7.

LA SCALA, ITALY

Today, our night-time city streets are full of electric light. Car headlights stream along the roads and neon signs buzz and flash all night long. Here in Dubai, the lights from stalls, hotels and lampposts shine on to the walkways.

DUBAI, UNITED ARAB EMIRATES

LIGHT POLLUTION

Electric light makes life easier and safer for humans, but too much of it is harmful to the environment. Light pollution – caused by an excess of artificial light – makes it difficult to see the stars and can affect the natural patterns of wildlife. Creatures like baby turtles or migrating birds can mistake electric light for moonlight, lose their way and become confused. Electric lights also disrupt our circadian rhythms (see page 78), making it harder for our body clocks to work out if it's night or day.

Cities at night aren't just bright – they can also be noisy. The beat of live music often carries on long after dark, at discos or concerts with flashing lights. Late-night dance lessons also use electric light, while some night-time festivals glow like rainbows.

ICE AND SNOW FESTIVAL, CHINA

Whizz! Bang! Not all human-made lights are electric, but they glow just as brightly. Fireworks were first invented in China more than 2,000 years ago. Today, on special occasions such as New Year's Eve, weddings and festivals, fireworks rocket into the night air, filling the sky with rainbow explosions.

DIWALI CELEBRATIONS, INDIA

WHO WORKS AT NIGHT?

Most people with jobs go to work during the day – but that's not true for everyone. All sorts of people are hard at work while you're asleep. In some countries, nearly a fifth of all workers do their jobs at night.

Some shops and petrol stations stay open for 24 hours a day, so that people awake at night can buy food and refuel their vehicles.

Hospitals needs to keep operating around the clock, caring for patients and handling emergencies. At night, teams of doctors, nurses and ambulance drivers take over from the teams who worked in the day. A night shift can last up to 12 hours.

Bakers need to start baking in the middle of the night to have bread and pastries to sell when people wake up for breakfast.

When office workers leave for the day, other staff are just starting. Security guards protect the building at night while cleaners get everything clean for the next day.

In the sorting office, postal workers are preparing the mail for the next day. Thousands of cards, letters and parcels have to be loaded on to mail vans for the morning.

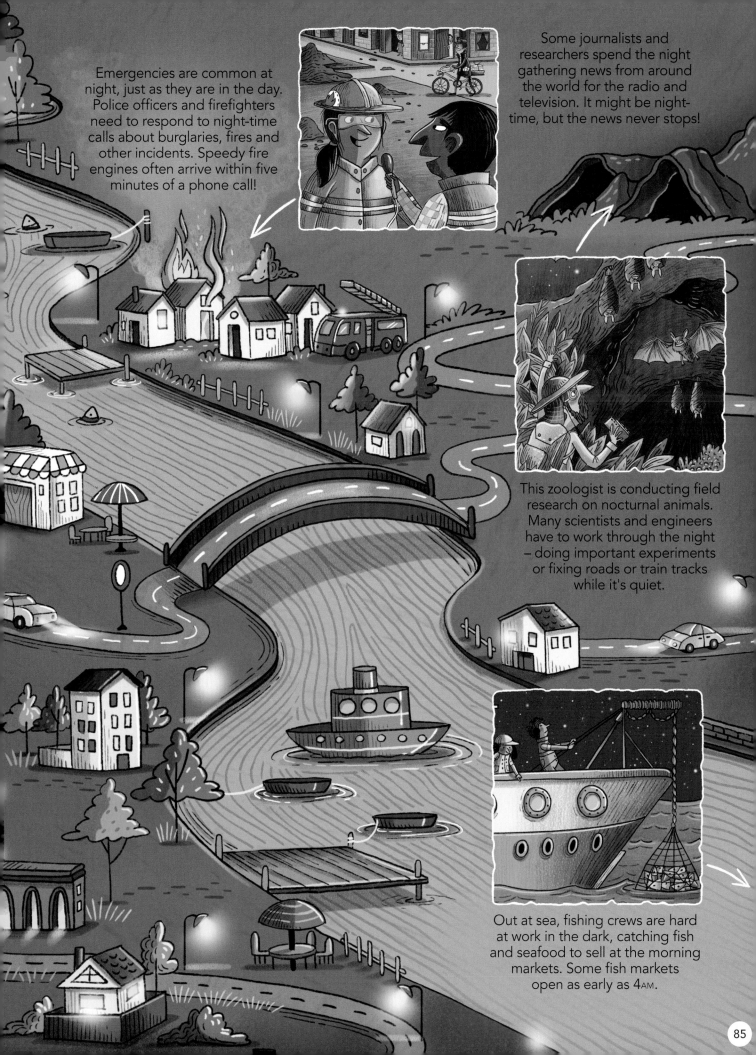

Emergencies are common at night, just as they are in the day. Police officers and firefighters need to respond to night-time calls about burglaries, fires and other incidents. Speedy fire engines often arrive within five minutes of a phone call!

Some journalists and researchers spend the night gathering news from around the world for the radio and television. It might be night-time, but the news never stops!

This zoologist is conducting field research on nocturnal animals. Many scientists and engineers have to work through the night – doing important experiments or fixing roads or train tracks while it's quiet.

Out at sea, fishing crews are hard at work in the dark, catching fish and seafood to sell at the morning markets. Some fish markets open as early as 4AM.

DAWN

It's early in the morning. Night-time is nearly over, and the skies are slowly starting to lighten. Minute by minute, the world outside is becoming clearer. This is the period that we call **dawn**.

Astronomical dawn officially begins when the centre of the Sun is 18 degrees below the horizon. It starts with a very gradual lightening of the sky. The Sun itself is still well below the horizon, so the light we see at first is weak and milky. The dawn becomes fuller and brighter as the Sun moves higher. Eventually, its fiery glow will break over the horizon.

HUMANS AT DAWN

For many of us, this time of day is hushed and quiet. Often, we're still asleep. But outside our bedrooms, lots of activity is taking place.

Many workers who have been awake all night are now heading home to rest. At the same time, some people who have been sleeping – such as farmers and café owners – are getting ready to start work early.

The animal kingdom is also busy. Around the world, some creatures, such as **badgers**, are returning to their dens and burrows, just as others are using the low light to hunt and forage.

DAWN CHORUS

Many bird species wake at dawn. They can be hard to see – but they're often easy to hear! When lots of birds are singing at the start of a new day, we describe it as a dawn chorus.

For birds, this is a good time of day to be noisy because it's not yet light enough for them to feed, or to be spotted by predators.

But why do they sing? Most of the dawn birdsong we hear comes from male birds. There are two main reasons why they sing. The first is to defend their territory. When they sing, they're sending a message that this area is theirs.

SONGTHRUSH

CHIFFCHAFF

BLACKBIRD

The second reason is to attract a partner. By singing loudly and clearly, male birds are displaying their strength and health to female birds. In many places, the dawn chorus is loudest in spring, when birds start building nests and having chicks. Sometimes, during dawn in the countryside, it's possible to hear hundreds of birds at the same time.

BLACKCAP

AS NIGHT TURNS TO DAY ...

Silently, slowly, the Sun creeps over the horizon. Rays of golden light wash across the land, bringing night to an end. Because of the way Earth rotates, the Sun always sets in the west and rises in the east.

The rich colours of sunrise are caused by the way sunlight gets scattered by droplets and tiny molecules in Earth's atmosphere. When the Sun is low on the horizon, sunlight needs to travel through a thick layer of atmosphere to reach us.

Sunlight is made of different colour wavelengths. In the early morning, the blue wavelengths get scattered more easily in the atmosphere, leaving us with reds, yellows and oranges.

As the Sun rises higher in the sky, a brand-new day is beginning. Nocturnal animals have taken themselves away to rest, while other creatures emerge into the heat and light of the morning.

All around the world, sunrise brings new life and new activity. The hours of darkness are over, and for many creatures it's now time to move around and look for food.

For more than four billion years, sunrise has brought daily light and warmth to the surface of the world. As morning breaks on Planet Earth, the great cycle of life continues.

GLOSSARY

ASTRONOMICAL SPRING / SUMMER / AUTUMN / WINTER
The four seasons, as determined by the tilt of Earth's axis and our movement around the Sun.

ASTRONOMY
The study of objects outside Earth's atmosphere, including stars, planets, galaxies and the wider universe.

AURORA AUSTRALIS
Also called the Southern Lights, a display of light caused by particles from the Sun hitting Earth's magnetic field. It's seen mostly in Antarctica and sometimes in other parts of the southern hemisphere.

AURORA BOREALIS
Also called the Northern Lights, a display of light caused by particles from the Sun hitting Earth's magnetic field. It's seen mostly in the Arctic and sometimes in other parts of the northern hemisphere.

AXIS
An imaginary line that an object, such as a planet, turns around.

BIOLUMINESCENCE
A natural light given off by a living creature, including some species of insect, fish, plankton, jellyfish or squid.

CIRCADIAN RHYTHM
A natural 24-hour pattern that almost all living things follow, which tells them when to sleep and when to wake.

CONES (IN THE EYE)
Cells inside a part of the eye called the retina that detect light and sense colour and detail. They work best in bright light.

CONSTELLATION
A group of stars that appears in a certain formation and has a name, such as Orion.

CREPUSCULAR
Describes animals that are active at twilight (dawn and dusk).

DAWN
The time when the sky starts to become lighter as the Sun rises. It officially starts when the Sun is 18 degrees below the horizon.

DIURNAL
Describes creatures that are mostly active during the day.

ECHOLOCATION
A technique which animals, such as bats and porpoises, use to find their way around and locate prey and other objects. They do this by producing sound waves that bounce back off anything they hit.

HABITAT
A place in the natural environment where an animal makes its home. Deserts and forests are two examples of habitats.

HIBERNATION
A resting and inactive state in which certain animals spend the winter, before emerging in spring.

HORIZON
The line in the distance where the sky and land seem to meet.

LUCIFERIN
A chemical compound which produces light when mixed with oxygen. It is found in bioluminescent organisms.

LUNAR ECLIPSE
During an eclipse, one object in space passes directly between two other objects, blocking their view of each other. In a lunar eclipse, Earth comes between the Sun and the Moon.

MIGRATION
When groups of animals travel large distances from one location to another at certain times of the year.

NOCTURNAL
Describes creatures that are awake at night but asleep during the day.

POLAR NIGHT
Occurring in winter in the Arctic and Antarctic Circles, this is the dark period when the Sun doesn't rise above the horizon for at least 24 hours – and sometimes many months. The closer to the Poles, the longer the polar night lasts.

POLLINATOR
Something which fertilizes a tree or plant with pollen, usually an insect.

PREDATOR
An animal that lives by killing and eating other animals.

REM (EYES)
An abbreviation of Rapid Eye Movement. REM sleep is a phase of sleep when someone's eyes move quickly under their eyelids, and dreams often happen.

RESPIRATION
When oxygen is absorbed by an organism and carbon dioxide is released as waste.

RETINA
A thin layer of tissue at the back of the eyeball that detects light and sends images to the brain, through a nerve called the optic nerve.

RODS (EYES)
Cells inside a part of the eye called the retina which sense shape and movement, and are vital for seeing in dim light.

TAPETUM LUCIDUM
A layer of tissue in the eye which acts like a mirror, reflecting light back into a part of the eye called the retina. It improves night vision. Many nocturnal animals have this feature.

TIDES (HIGH)
When the water level in oceans and seas rises and the water travels further inland because of the influence of the Moon. High tides happen twice in every 24-hour period.

TIDES (LOW)
When the water level in seas and oceans falls and the water travels away from land, revealing more of the shore. Low tide happens twice in each 24-hour period and is caused by the influence of the Moon.

TOTAL SOLAR ECLIPSE
During an eclipse, one object in space passes directly between two other objects, blocking their view of each other. During a total solar eclipse, the Moon comes between the Sun and the Earth, blocking the view of the Sun from Earth.

TWILIGHT
The faint light that can be seen after sunset when the Sun has set below the horizon, or just before dawn when it is about to rise.

INDEX

ABOUT BEN AND PAULA

Ben Lerwill is an award-winning travel writer and author living in a small village in England. He's crept through the Amazon Rainforest in the dark, watched the Northern Lights over Arctic Norway and taken more overnight trains than he can remember. He used to work at night stacking shelves for a DIY store and his favourite constellation is Cassiopeia.

Paula Bossio is an award-winning Colombian illustrator and author, whose work has been published all over the world. She sees the mysterious beauty of night in a firefly's magical sparkle, and in the scent of night-blooming jasmine at dusk, which reminds her fondly of her childhood. In particular, she loves the opportunity that darkness brings to gather around a warm fire with her loved ones.